HOW TO BE A...

CHAP

HOW TO BE A... CHAP

Copyright © Summersdale Publishers Ltd, 2014

Text by Chris Turton
Cover and page designs by Mr Bliss
Icons © Shutterstock
Main illustrations by Adam Nickel

Summersdale Publishers Ltd
46 West Street
Chichester
West Sussex
PO19 1RP
UK

www.summersdale.com

Printed and bound in China

ISBN: 978-1-84953-587-8

Substantial discounts on bulk quantities of Summersdale books are available to corporations, professional associations and other organisations. For details contact Nicky Douglas by telephone: +44 (0) 1243 756902, fax: +44 (0) 1243 786300 or email: nicky@summersdale.com.

HOW TO BE A...

CHAP

A Nifty Guide for Top-Notch Gents

Illustrations by
Adam Nickel

Dickie Archer

summersdale

*To all practitioners
in the art of being
a Gentleman*

CONTENTS

Introduction...7

The Look

Coiffure...10
Attire..14
Accessories...22
Transport...28

The Character

Parlance...36
Music..42
Literature...50
Film...56

In Practice

Etiquette...64
Courting...70
Carousing...74

INTRODUCTION

WELCOME, GENTLEMEN, to *How to Be a... Chap*, your nifty pocket guide to all matters relating to the art of vintage style and genteel comportment! This book is intended to offer friendly advice that might help one to achieve the look, attitude and general sophistications of that increasingly endangered species known as the Gentleman.

But what exactly is a 'Chap'? Most dictionaries offer the definition as 'man or boy', which says little of the connotations of refinement that the term evokes. A Chap is a 'good egg'; a 'fine sort'; a man of special qualities which are reflected in the way he looks and in the way he acts.

Although this book takes its inspiration from fashions and mores of bygone eras (specifically the forties and fifties), these ideas will be used purely - often with tongue in cheek - as inspiration, rather than as reiterations of lamentable attitudes towards what one 'should' and 'shouldn't' do.

In this author's humble opinion, what truly defines a man as a Chap is not acquiring a millimetre-perfect moustache or exquisitely tailored suit, in some vain attempt to out-dapper one's fellow man; but rather, the desire to act with good form and grace in all situations. A Chap is masterful enough to show refinement but brave enough not to be unnecessarily constrained by ceremony – to have the wits to know how to act with class but to have the imagination not to be limited by it.

Above all of the specific assertions made in this book regarding the superficial refinements of a Chap, one thought should remain within the reader's mind:

A Chap is, in essence…

Charming
Honest
Attentive
Presentable

With that idea firmly planted, let us proceed!

CHAP

The Look

THE MARK of a true Chap is in his heart
rather than his hatband, granted – but, like the
peacock, he is most readily identified by his
elaborate plumage: a smoothly styled side-
parting in his hair; a flash of silken paisley
in his cravat and the twinkle of his cufflinks.
These things, along with numerous other
adornments, constitute the image of the Chap.

A golden rule to keep in mind: if you're aiming
for a full-on vintage get-up – be it drawing-
room casual with dressing gown, pipe and
slippers, or dining-room chic with bow tie and
tux – be sure to execute the look coherently
and consistently, with *every item* in keeping
with the style you're aiming to achieve.

THE HAIR - on one's head and on one's upper lip - is where the Chap is first established. Hairstyles express just as much about one's character as any other facet of the Chap style, especially since this is the one area which is not stitched, starched or shined into shape. That said, the aspiring gent may turn to many 'classic' styles to achieve a look that is suitably suave. When choosing, consider that a hairstyle should suit the shape of one's face: for those gents with a rounder face, an upright style such as a brushed-back side parting with short back and sides will work nicely, whereas those fellows with a thinner visage can look smart with a wider, flatter style such as a centre parting. Whichever you choose, some kind of pomade (Brylcreem, etc.) is essential. As for that king of hirsute adornments - the moustache - choices are many; this is where a man can add a real touch of retro flair to his look, as we shall see.

Classic Hairstyles

The Side Parting

Everyone has a natural parting in their hair which can be followed when creating a side parting. The style harks back to the twenties and before, popularised by silver screen Chaps like Rudolph Valentino. Whichever side the hair is parted on, it should be cut relatively short and combed, with the help of a quality pomade, so it lies quite flat against the top of the head.

The Slick-Back

A staple of men's fashion is the slick-back – quite simply, hair combed back in a neat and orderly fashion and set with a pomade. This is not to be confused with the more flamboyant American 'pompadour' style, sported  by so many rabble-rousing Teddy boys in fifties Britain. However, today the 'quiff' does not have such associations, and therefore - if cut to a conservative length – can be understated yet impressive.

The Centre Parting

Parted in the centre, yes, but not draped over the forehead. As with the slick-back, hair may be brushed back, but this time parted sharply and equally down the centre.

Hairstyles are one way to exhibit one's basic Chap credentials, but the almighty moustache is a bristled badge of honour. For the aspiring Chap – of yesteryear and of today – the moustache suggests tempered virility and crafted flair – a moustache is manly, but cultivated. So too is our Chap.

Chap Fact

Moustache hair grows faster than any other hair on the body. It sprouts more in spring and summer than in autumn and winter.

ATTIRE

GENTLEMANLY ATTIRE is an area in which the refinements of the Chap are allowed to unfurl like the petals of a sweet *boutonniere* (lapel flower). Clothes do not maketh the man, but they speak volumes of his personality; for the Chap, the message that comes from his attire should be well-rounded and confident, and not without an element of flair.

Again, there are many time-honoured styles for the aspiring Chap to seize upon, but perhaps what really distinguishes a genuine gent from the run-of-the-mill retro rookie is attention to detail: relative authenticity in fabric, colour and cut will make the difference when selecting clothing (as opposed to a modern 'reworking'). Furthermore, getting a distinguished look need not mean splashing out on Savile Row – looking spiffing is arguably more a case of careful selection (with the aforementioned criteria in mind) and so may be quite possible to achieve via the high street.

Shirts, Stockings and Other Particulars

The white dress shirt is perhaps the most essential piece of clothing in a Chap's wardrobe - a crisp, clean canvas onto which one may express oneself in broad or delicate strokes. Collar style is one aspect which can create an individual touch, albeit a subtle one.

Stockings (socks) will not make or break a look, though for the sake of coherence - and your own sense of pride - they should at least coordinate, in terms of colour, with your outfit.

As for other undergarments, comfort is practically the only thing that counts; though this is not a reason to opt for something distasteful!

Jackets and Trousers

There are far too many aspects to the sacred art of men's tailoring to cover the subject properly here – nonetheless, a useful tip to remember, if you have not chosen to wear a two- or three-piece suit, is that fabrics of jacket and trousers should complement each other, but need not be the same, e.g. if you're aiming for a country-casual look, coarse, textured fabrics like tweed and corduroy work perfectly – they create an interesting visual contrast but are also in the same sartorial family.

Cardigans

Not just for university professors and librarians, oh no! A fine cardigan can complement a jacket and trouser combination wonderfully, in a similar way to a waistcoat. The 'rule' of not fastening the bottom button need not apply to cardigans - indeed, it can look untidy! Chunky-knit cardies are likely to be too bulky underneath jackets, so opt for something thinner and with small, understated buttons.

Suits

The crowning glory of the Chap's ensemble is the suit; nothing looks more dapper. Again, there are many classic styles, but whichever one you choose, be mindful of colour and fabric: a sharply cut, shiny, metallic-look jacket and trousers will not ooze vintage charm. That said, one thing is even more important: fit; there is little worse than an ill-fitting suit, even if it is perfect in every other way. The staple of the contemporary Chap is arguably the single-breasted jacket and trousers or 'lounge' suit. A rule of thumb for this type of suit is: always fasten the middle button when standing, and unfasten it when sitting down – leave the bottom button unfastened at all times! This will ensure you keep your suit true to its cut and shape without looking trussed up like a Christmas turkey.

Shoes

Classic styles abound here too: the Oxford, the Derby, the Loafer - the list goes on. Shoes are perhaps one area in which one cannot compromise on quality (and, therefore price); they may be the last thing one notices when taking in the splendiferous ensemble of a finely clothed gent, but they are no less important for it. Many an aspiring Chap is let down by substandard footwear which he has wrongly presumed to be insignificant. Outside of colour coordination, consider how 'showy' the shoe is - a pair of full brogues with intricate decoration, for instance, may make your outfit too busy.

'The boor covers himself, the rich man or the fool adorns himself, and the elegant man gets dressed.'

Honoré de Balzac

ACCESSORIES ARE the finishing touches to a look and separate the natty from the newbie. A man in a suit is just that; a man in a suit with an elegant pocket square, snap-brim fedora and stately wristwatch is a top-notch Chap. Again, the rule of consistency applies: a digital Japanese watch will do nothing but clash horribly with your antique cufflinks, therefore when choosing your accessories aim for items that are in keeping with the vintage style of your outfit. Aside from being extra style details in your ensemble, most gents' accessories have a practical purpose, so don't be daunted by the notion that you're being overly fancy with your tie clip or your Albert chain.

Ties and Handkerchiefs

A tie is an accent piece for your outfit; a voice which may declare your character and sartorial leanings in shouts or whispers. The handkerchief is the echo of this declaration – it need not be as loud but it must be faithful to the original utterance. When choosing a tie and hanky for your outfit, some degree of contrast in pattern, colour and material is often preferable – the pairing of a striped shirt and a striped tie, for instance, will be far too busy, and your handkerchief need only complement your tie, rather than match it exactly.

The tone of your tie should also be in tune with your ensemble: neckties are sharp and confident; cravats are frivolous yet sophisticated and bow ties are playful.

Jewellery

Every Chap should be punctual, so a wrist- or pocket-watch is all but essential. For wristwatches, be mindful of the strap colour and remember that something a little different – a square or oblong face, for instance – makes for an interesting talking point. The pocket watch is designed to be worn with a waistcoat, of course, and so is less versatile as a style object than the wristwatch.

Cufflinks, to be worn with a double-cuff shirt, are an especially nice touch, and ideally should be made of gold, silver or some other precious metal. Tie pins are arguably more of a novelty and so perhaps not quite as chic as the generally more understated tie clip.

Hats

Hats are another heritage item, the styles of which have been firmly established for decades, so guidelines on how to wear them are well documented. A bowler, for instance, suits a more business-type suit, whereas the flat cap naturally has more of a practical, country look. It can be tricky to find a hat that suits, however, as with hairstyles, the shape of one's face must be taken into account – a rounder face will be complemented by a taller hat, whereas a thinner face will suit a flatter one.

Umbrellas

Not only is an umbrella the most convenient way of staying dry while out and about, they are a wonderful prop for a stately stroll (especially when combined with a bowler!). The crook-handled, full-length stick umbrella is perhaps the most fitting for the Chap about town and a neutral colour – black or grey – will not detract from your outfit.

Chap Fact

Samuel Fox, born in Bradwell in Derby, England, is widely recognised as the inventor of the modern, steel-framed umbrella (1851). Fox Umbrellas are still available today.

TRANSPORT

STROLLING LEISURELY in all your Chap finery is surely a delight, however there may come a point when vehicular comportment is preferable – not only for convenience, but for the sake of preserving one's clothing and of course one's dashing, debonair image. Indeed, Chaps throughout the ages have been just as drawn to Ferraris as they have to fedoras – history is replete with gallant racing-car drivers, pilots and the like. The 'classic' car offers not only the opportunity to travel in vintage style, but also a chance to don more gentlemanly attire.

Today's Chap has many more options open to him with bicycles and public transportation, such as trains and taxis.

Bicycle

Since John Kemp Starley established the Rover Safety cycle in 1885, the bicycle has been wholeheartedly embraced as a relatively cheap and supremely efficient mode of personal transport. Cheap and easy does not mean that the bicycle lacks dignity; many elegant, vintage-inspired models are readily available today, as are a host of bespoke retro accessories. At the very least, travelling by bicycle will afford the more adventurous Chap the opportunity to adorn himself with plus fours, high socks and flat cap – sporty and spiffing!

Motor Car

Cruising along a country lane, accompanied by a beloved friend or 'amour', with the sun on one's face and the wind in one's hair is an experience that many a Gentleman longs for. The vintage romance of such a scene is largely dependent on the calibre of your vehicle – not the cubic capacity of the engine but the prestige of the car itself: sadly, a Vauxhall Nova with a go-faster stripe and ear-piercing exhaust muffler will not cut the Chap mustard! That said, a truly stunning vintage car is something that is only readily available for those persons with a large amount of disposable income. Less luxurious, but still technically 'classic', models might partly live up to the dream, but keep in mind the old motto: if something is worth doing, it's worth doing well.

Classic Motor Vehicles of the Twentieth Century

Here's a selection of vintage vehicles to make any aspiring Chap's eyes water:

- Jaguar E-Type
- Mercedes Benz 300 SL Coupe Gullwing
- Aston Martin DB5
- Morgan 4/4
- Rolls-Royce Phantom
- MGB
- Austin-Healey 3000 Mark III
- Triumph Spitfire
- Ferrari 275 GTB
- Porsche 356 Speedster

Locomotive

Passenger trains are not only a proud part of modern transport heritage; they are the epitome of relaxed, leisurely conveyance of the kind that all true Gentlemen relish. Travelling by steam locomotive – now arguably more of a novelty than a

Chap Fact

Sir John Betjeman, English poet, locomotive enthusiast and veritable Chap, is immortalised with a statue at St Pancras station, London.

necessity – is quintessentially Chap and allows one to partake in any number of edifying activities as lush, green countryside rolls slowly by outside the window – marvellous indeed.

'What Englishman will give his mind to politics as long as he can afford to keep a motor car?'

George Bernard Shaw

The Character

THE DEBONAIR look of a gentleman is necessarily complemented by a charming and cheerful character – giving substance to your style.

Without wanting to expound too forcefully the stereotypes which might make up the 'proper' character of a Chap – we are each, after all, individuals with countless facets to our personalities that should not be faked or falsified – this section presents some typically Chappish persuasions in the areas of parlance, music, literature and film.

PARLANCE

A REFINED vocabulary is something that adds to the quirky charm of the Chap persona, much of which naturally stems from polite and good-natured conversation. At the forefront of gentlemanly speech is courtesy, but this does not mean it cannot be playful or eloquent. Popular words and phrases do of course change through the decades, but there's something about the slightly silly yet highly inventive parlance of the British upper-classes during the forties and fifties that appeals, especially as today it has, arguably, lost all its pomp and pretension.

A Selection of Chap Phrases

The art of Chappish banter only really comes alive when in full swing, so here are some examples of conversational phrases in action (exaggerated for purposes of illustration – not recommended for actual use, unless at a fancy-dress party as Terry-Thomas):

'I say, my good man, did you happen to catch that BBC documentary on the development of the Corby trouser press last night? Jolly good, if I do say so myself.'

'Afternoon tea at Mrs Crumb's Crumpet Emporium at two, right-o!'

'Hard cheese, my dear fellow! A little quicker off the mark and you would've returned that volley, I dare say.'

'Poor show, old boy, poor show. Every man and his dog knows that the cigars are brought out *after* the brandy is served.'

Many a famous Chap exemplified his wit and wisdom with a quotable phrase or two – here are some of the finest:

'A gentleman is one who puts more into the world than he takes out.'

George Bernard Shaw

'It is not what he has, or even what he does which expresses the worth of a man, but what he is.'

Henri Frédéric Amiel

'Do something every day that you don't want to do; this is the golden rule for acquiring the habit of doing your duty without pain.'

Mark Twain

'The trouble with the world is that the stupid are cocksure and the intelligent are full of doubt.'

Bertrand Russell

'Some are blessed with musical ability, others with good looks. Myself, I was blessed with modesty.'

Roger Moore

'A man always has two reasons for what he does – a good one and the real one.'

J. P. Morgan

'When people tell you how young you look, they are telling you how old you are.'

Cary Grant

BEING FAMILIAR with the delightful nuances of music of a certain substance is a coup for any aspiring Chap - the effortless yet vibrant piano jazz of Dave Brubeck; the soaring strings of one of Mendelssohn's symphonies; the rich, sonorous vocals of Maria Callas - all of these things excite the intellect as well as the eardrums, and provide entertainment as well as talking points at a soirée or other such event. Choice of music is, of course, a deeply personal taste and that should not be compromised for any minor whim - however, there is always room for more music in the aficionado's collection, some of which may be of special interest to the Chap.

The Art of Vinyl

In the age of digital recording, one may expect that the vinyl record has been consigned to the museum – this is of course far from the truth! The LP is alive and kicking and offers a unique and nostalgic listening experience. Even the most average of album sleeves looks crafted; the glossy black discs are a pleasure to carefully position onto the turntable and the sound is full and alive. These things combine to make a classy listening experience – one that is more involved and attention-holding, demanding knowledge and refinements all its own. This, together with the selection of some stimulating music, cannot fail to reflect well on a man of good taste.

Cool Grooves and Delightful Ditties

Jazz is known for being a distinctly American art form, yet there have been, and still are, many proponents from all over the globe. Jazz numbers can sometimes unravel into complex musical exercises, so for a relaxed yet stimulating ambiance, pass over the Coltrane and head to Chet Baker or Bill Evans; or Duke Ellington or Humphrey Lyttelton for jumping and jiving.

Vocal artists, that is, singers who are best known for their singing rather than anything else, are instantly agreeable - it's hard to object to a wonderful voice, regardless of personal tastes. Many of the greats could sing in any number of styles, yet for the home setting the velvety tones of Nat King Cole or Ella Fitzgerald are guaranteed to please.

Orchestral music can be soothing or scintillating (or both!), depending on the musicians and the numbers they play. This type of music demands proper appreciation and therefore can prove a challenge to the casual listener so, if you opt to dust off your Rachmaninoff, try to be sure it will be well received.

'For me, music and life are all about style.'

Miles Davis

Chap Musicians and Singers

Count Basie
William James Basie was an African-American musician best known for leading his jazz orchestra in performances in the thirties and forties – he acquired the name 'Count' after a club announcer insisted that he, like his contemporaries Duke Ellington and Earl Hines, deserved a regal-sounding moniker.

Louis Armstrong
This unforgettable African-American trumpet player, nicknamed Satchmo, was a larger-than-life character and just as well known for his unique vocal sound as for his playing. A remarkable performer and a true Gentleman.

Django Reinhardt

Jean Reinhardt was another jazz great – a Belgian-born guitarist who, at the age of 18, lost the use of two of his fingers. Despite his injury, he went on to become an exemplary guitarist and is regarded as one of the greats. His nickname, in the Romani language, means 'I awake'.

Frank Sinatra

Ol' Blue Eyes needs no introduction – his reputation as a singer with effortless style and charm was thoroughly deserved. A coquettish character on stage and on screen, he will forever be remembered as the ultimate crooner.

A WELL-READ gentleman is never short on interesting conversation; he knows how to use his imagination and has a world of intriguing places, characters and ideas to draw upon. These are all fine things for a Chap to have at his command. The literary universe may provide inspiration in practically every aspect of life, not least in the area of Chapness: consider the brazen allure of Jay Gatsby; the intellectual cunning of Sherlock Holmes or the frivolous indulgence of Dorian Gray – not all of the examples one may find are commendable in a real-life context, but if nothing else they provoke creative thinking and new ideas.

The Library Of Chap

A Good Read

All works of literature enrich the reader in some way - here's a selection which may assist in a Chap's general edification:

The Odyssey by Homer
In this ancient tale of one man's epic journey to reach his homeland the central character of Odysseus is far from perfect - he is sometimes brash and boastful and is defined as having a 'cunning intelligence' - yet one of his outstanding traits is perseverance; the will to never give up despite an obscene amount of bad luck and setbacks.

Chap factor: 5/10 - an unforgettable tale of heroism, but one whose central character is flawed and sporting sandals.

Shakespeare's Collected Works

There is everyday eloquence and there is Shakespearean eloquence. Although many of his plays feature deplorable villains and horrific tragedies, the Bard's work is some of the finest poetry ever written, full to the brim with gloriously cadenced witticisms and of the sort that even the most switched-on of gentlemen will forever envy. He's also responsible for coining many Chappish terms, including 'fancy-free', 'for goodness' sake' and 'in a pickle'.

Chap Factor: 7/10 – the ruff may never come back into style, but Old Bill's poetry and prose will live forever.

A Study in Scarlet by Arthur Conan Doyle

The inimitable Gentleman sleuth Sherlock Holmes first appeared formally in this 1887 novel. As well as having a remarkable wardrobe, his character is a first-class example of composure, eloquence and intelligence. He is also an aficionado of the pipe – not as popular today but nonetheless quintessentially Chap.

Chap Factor: 9/10 – One of the first fictional Chaps – a high score is elementary!

The Wind in the Willows by Kenneth Grahame

Aside from having a moustache that could cause the most facially hirsute Chap to weep with jealousy, this outstanding Edwardian author is responsible for a classic tale of friendship and harmonious living. His characters embody many different human traits, but all are incredibly Chappish: Mr Toad is flamboyant, Ratty is cultured, Mole is mild-mannered and Mr Badger is wise. As well as this, the book reminds us that rivers and trees are as important as Brylcreem and bow ties.

Chap Factor: 8/10 – an admirable collection of fine, furry gentle-beasts.

Chap Fact

Sherlock Holmes is in fact never explicitly described as wearing a deerstalker hat in the Conan Doyle novels, only an 'ear-flapped travelling cap'.

THE SILVER screen has been and will perhaps always be wrought with handsome, stylish Chaps of every sort. In the early days of cinema simply appearing before an audience on a big screen was enough to cause excitement, but when the glamour of the Hollywood studio system set in the stars shone brighter than ever. Tales of dashing, death-defying secret agents, noble, heartfelt romantics and cheeky and charming men-about-town were abundant – all of which were thoroughly entertaining exaggerations of your regular Chap and most were thoroughly imitable. Many unforgettable characters were immortalised in the movies, be it through their memorable outfits, impressive mannerisms or simply for delivering a monumental line.

Classic Chaps of the Silver Screen

Terry-Thomas

Terry-Thomas enjoyed many appearances in British studio comedies such as *School for Scoundrels* and *Make Mine Mink* and is perhaps best remembered for his roles as the typical English 'bounder' or 'cad'. Despite being typecast as a rotten sort, Terry always seemed to be immaculately turned out, both on screen and off, and was a genuine Chap.

Chap Weapon of Choice: the 7-inch cigarette holder

Sean Connery

Sean Connery has had many memorable roles, but as obvious as it is it's hard to ignore his incarnation as Agent 007. Connery was the first to give James Bond a presence on the silver screen in *Dr No*, with swarthy good looks, a strong yet smooth voice and a killer wardrobe. Not only did he look good, he saved the world and got the girls; a playboy on Her Majesty's payroll.

Chap Weapon of Choice: the Martini - shaken, not stirred

Cary Grant

As memorable in his Hitchcock films, such as *North By Northwest*, as in his romcom roles, such as *Charade* with Audrey Hepburn, Cary Grant established himself as an actor of broad and remarkable talent, second only to Humphrey Bogart in the list of Greatest Male Stars of All Time, according to the AFI. His popularity eventually preceded him, as he was famously quoted as saying: 'Everyone wants to be Cary Grant. Even I want to be Cary Grant.'

Chap Weapon of Choice: the piercing, stern-sexy stare

Clark Gable

Gable had a long and illustrious career as a leading man in over 60 movies, hence his nickname The King of Hollywood. Arguably, his most famous role was as Rhett Butler in the historical romance feature *Gone with the Wind*. At the end of the film he delivers one of the most quoted lines in movie history (and one that is entirely Chap, despite the period setting): 'Frankly, my dear...' (You know the rest!)

Chap Weapon of Choice: a razor-sharp moustache

'I'm no actor and I never have been. What people see on the screen is me.'

Clark Gable

In Practice

YOU MAY have perfected styling your retro do, achieved sartorial excellence, got your lingo down pat and absorbed all the Chappish wisdom your local library shelves have to offer; but all of this is worth nothing unless you can conduct yourself in a genteel way while going about your everyday business. Any slap-dash bounder with a 'tache can look the part, but it takes a true gentleman to exude class and composure when faced with the countless little challenges life throws at him.

TO SOME, 'etiquette' is a dirty word. This is somewhat understandable, as it has connotations of unnecessary rules devised in the days when society was so uptight that one could barely blink without the proper say-so. However, at the heart of etiquette is simple, shared politeness to one's fellow man and woman, with a bit of added flair to make things seem more special. There is something deeply satisfying in partaking in formal social rituals, perhaps because it acts as a more definite reminder that we are civilised beings – those who can freely enjoy sumptuous dinners, fine cigars and a damn good snifter of cognac brandy!

Greetings

A firm handshake or three is the hallmark of a top-notch fellow, when greeting old friends and new – so too is the friendly smile and direct eye-contact. A pat on the back if the person be well known to you drives the sentiment home. The vigorous handshake is perhaps less often employed when greeting a lady, but this may depend on the situation and the person. The old-fashioned approach is to offer one's hand, slightly upturned, and to give a more restrained single shake. This may be accompanied by a single peck on the cheek or with the free hand being placed on top of the clasped hand if the lady is familiar.

Dining

Dining in a formal setting, perhaps more than any other area of social engagement, has more rules than one can shake a stick at! Here are some golden rules that will most likely see you through most situations:

1. Stand up for a new person joining or leaving the table.

2. Refrain from eating until everyone else is ready.

3. Always offer to serve others – with wine, water, etc. – before yourself.

4. If you're a guest, pay your host the courtesy of finishing eating after or at the same time as them.

5. Excuse yourself when leaving the table before the food is finished.

Chap Fact

Amuse-bouche (those little appetisers that are often served before a gourmet meal) translates literally as 'mouth-amuser'.

Small Talk

Small talk is not simply for killing time in awkward situations – it can break the ice and is a gateway into more meaningful conversation. In this respect it's essential in bridging a gap between new acquaintances in any situation; and if nothing else, it's an excuse to be witty and charming! A good starting point is to remark upon something that is commonly shared – the weather, for instance – or, if you're feeling up to it, a compliment. The key is to be attentive and appear interested when you get a response, and to keep the momentum of the conversation going, so avoiding one-word answers is a must.

Goodbyes

Saying farewell may run quite similarly to saying hello – a handshake or a peck on the cheek, depending on the feel you get from a new acquaintance. If you're at a social gathering and you feel it's time to depart, do so with confidence – that is, try not to dilly-dally: make your intentions known politely (perhaps even with a bit of humour thrown in), thank your host and say your goodbyes to friends.

Here are a few Chappish salutations which may fit the bill:

So long!

Toodle pip!

COURTING

COURTING, THE art of romance, is something that can arguably only be learned the hard way, by making one's own mistakes, however, it certainly doesn't hurt to get some pointers in this most delicate of areas. Being polite and courteous will go some way in making a positive impression on a first date, for instance, but overdoing the knight-in-shining-armour routine can be off-putting in all sorts of ways. One mustn't be afraid to assert one's personality, above and beyond the 'please's and 'thank you's – this is, after all, what makes us individuals. There are tasteful ways of doing this, though.

Here are some general **DOs** and **DON'Ts** which may be of some use when in the company of the object of your affection, especially early on:

DO assert yourself in conversation.

DON'T dominate the conversation to the point at which your date begins to look uninterested.

DO make positive eye contact when being spoken to.

DON'T let your eyes wander to inappropriate parts of their body.

DO present yourself as witty and intelligent when speaking.

DON'T use bad language, bad jokes or controversial subject areas for effect.

DO reciprocate if your date initiates any tender physical contact.

DON'T become too familiar too soon – and don't feel pressured to become intimate for the sake of ceremony.

DO conduct yourself in a courteous manner.

DON'T overdo your chivalry – ideally, although the offer can always be there, a bill (as well as everything else) should be shared equally.

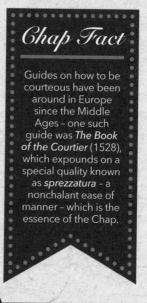

Chap Fact

Guides on how to be courteous have been around in Europe since the Middle Ages – one such guide was *The Book of the Courtier* (1528), which expounds on a special quality known as *sprezzatura* – a nonchalant ease of manner – which is the essence of the Chap.

CAROUSING

WHAT IS life without celebration? Everyone - Chap or no - needs time to be footloose and fancy-free. However, reckless abandon should not be in the Gentleman's behavioural vocabulary. There is classy celebration and outright indulgence, and the latter is to be avoided. Enjoyment of food, fine wines and frolics is something to be relished at a civilised pace; this is aided by little formalities, which make each of these things a miniature event in itself.

As many a wise mother has iterated: 'A little bit of what you fancy is good for you.'

Alcohol

Many are the delights of alcohol: amber Scotches, ruby ports, silvery gins, emerald absinthe; the list goes on. The world of fine wines and liqueurs is a wonderful cornucopia, from the elegant bottles and artful labels to the curiously shaped glasses in which the drinks are served and, indeed, the intriguing ways that have been devised to serve them. We drink to celebrate and to commiserate, and there are few events in life for which some reason for a drink cannot be found. As such, there is little point in attempting to even scratch the surface of the wherefores of drink in the context of the gent – instead, your author will simply offer this pearl of wisdom from proto-Chap Samuel Johnson:

'Claret is the liquor for boys, port for men; but he who aspires to be a hero must drink brandy.'

Tobacco

Smoking is generally frowned upon nowadays, as the threats to one's health are undeniable – however it has had a strong connection to the Chap image throughout history, especially so with the humble (or, in the case of Sherlock Holmes, rather ornate) pipe. There is a unique finery that comes with smoking – the rich, earthy-herbal smell of tobacco is a joy to some, as is the ritual of 'toasting the foot' of a chunky Cuban cigar before reposing for an hour or two, gently blowing grey-blue smoke into the air. Indeed, smoking is a perfect waste of time, entertained purely for its own sake, and in this respect it is as pointless as it is marvellous. And if you're keen to indulge this habit without putting a dent in your rude health in the process, there's always tobacco substitute!

Dancing

Dancing affords the aspiring Chap many opportunities - a chance to enjoy the close company of a dancing partner and to display his graceful tendencies and refinements, or to simply enjoy himself in the movement and music. It's not all about swanning around the ballroom: a Chap should be able to turn his feet, hands and hips to something more upbeat like the jitterbug or the twist. Either way, it will pay to become proficient in one or the other - or both!

Congratulations, dear fellow!

You have reached the end of this nifty little guide. I sincerely hope it has been informative in its own small way. The art of the Gentleman is one that cannot be mastered easily or quickly; but stick at it – a little bit of Chap goes a long way, and the endeavour is truly worthwhile. And remember, being a Chap is about maintaining good form in all situations – which includes having fun!

Yours in Chapness,

Dickie Archer

If you're interested in finding out more about our books, find us on Facebook at **Summersdale Publishers** and follow us on **Twitter** at **@Summersdale**.

www.summersdale.com